# TV **COOKS**

Nick Nairn

# *The Main Course*

BBC BOOKS

Published by BBC Books,
an imprint of BBC Worldwide Limited,
Woodlands, 80 Wood Lane, London W12 0TT.

The recipes in this book first appeared in:
**Wild Harvest with Nick Nairn**
© Nick Nairn 1996
**Wild Harvest 2**
© Nick Nairn 1997

This edition first published 1998
Recipes © Nick Nairn 1998
The moral right of the author has been asserted
Photographs by Juliet Piddington © BBC Worldwide
Limited 1997
Author photograph © Graham Lees

ISBN 0 563 38412 3

Edited by Pam Mallender
Designed by Sarah Amit
Styling by Juliet Piddington and Jane Parry
Home Economist Sarah Ramsbottom

Set in New Caledonia and Helvetica
Printed and bound in France by
Imprimerie Pollina s.a.
Colour separations by Imprimerie Pollina s.a.
Cover printed by Imprimerie Pollina s.a.

Cover and frontispiece: North African Couscous
with Roast Vegetables

## CONTENTS

# RECIPE NOTES

Eggs are medium. If your kitchen is warm, keep the eggs in the fridge, but allow them to come to room temperature before using.
Wash all fresh produce before preparation and peel as necessary.
Spoon measurements are level. Always use proper measuring spoons:
1 teaspoon = 5ml and 1 tablespoon = 15ml.
Never mix metric and imperial measures in one recipe. Stick to one or the other.

# HANDY CONVERSION TABLES

| Weight | | Volume | | Linear | |
|---|---|---|---|---|---|
| 15g | ½oz | 30ml | 1fl oz | 5mm | ¼in |
| 25g | 1oz | 50ml | 2fl oz | 10mm/1cm | ½in |
| 40g | 1½oz | 100ml | 3½fl oz | 2cm | ¾in |
| 55g | 2oz | 125ml | 4fl oz | 2.5cm | 1in |
| 85g | 3oz | 150ml | 5fl oz (¼ pint) | 5cm | 2in |
| 115g | 4oz | 175ml | 6fl oz | 7.5cm | 3in |
| 140g | 5oz | 200ml | 7fl oz (⅓ pint) | 10cm | 4in |
| 175g | 6oz | 225ml | 8fl oz | 13cm | 5in |
| 200g | 7oz | 250ml | 9fl oz | 15cm | 6in |
| 225g | 8oz | 300ml | 10fl oz (½ pint) | 18cm | 7in |
| 250g | 9oz | 350ml | 12fl oz | 20cm | 8in |
| 280g | 10oz | 400ml | 14fl oz | 23cm | 9in |
| 350g | 12oz | 425ml | 15fl oz (¾ pint) | 25cm | 10in |
| 375g | 13oz | 450ml | 16fl oz | 28cm | 11in |
| 400g | 14oz | 500ml | 18fl oz | 30cm | 12in |
| 425g | 15oz | 600ml | 20fl oz (1 pint) | | |
| 450g | 1lb | 700ml | 1¼ pints | | |
| 550g | 1¼lb | 850ml | 1½ pints | | |
| 750g | 1lb 10oz | 1 litre | 1¾ pints | | |
| 900g | 2lb | 1.2 litres | 2 pints | | |
| 1kg | 2¼lb | 1.3 litres | 2¼ pints | | |
| 1.3kg | 3lb | 1.4 litres | 2½ pints | | |
| 1.8kg | 4lb | 1.7 litres | 3 pints | | |
| 2.25kg | 5lb | 2 litres | 3½ pints | | |
| | | 2.5 litres | 4½ pints | | |

**Oven temperatures**

| | | |
|---|---|---|
| 225F | 110C | GAS ¼ |
| 250F | 120C | GAS ½ |
| 275F | 140C | GAS 1 |
| 300F | 150C | GAS 2 |
| 325F | 160C | GAS 3 |
| 350F | 180C | GAS 4 |
| 375F | 190C | GAS 5 |
| 400F | 200C | GAS 6 |
| 425F | 220C | GAS 7 |
| 450F | 230C | GAS 8 |
| 475F | 240C | GAS 9 |

Ⓥ    **Suitable for vegetarians**

❉    **Suitable for freezing**

The main course is the centre-piece of any meal; your crowning glory, a demonstration of just what a canny knack you have in the kitchen or, if you lead a fast and furious life, the main meal of your day – something to settle down to and enjoy. Either way the main course has to be the one that you put the most time and effort into.

Depending on who, and what, it's for, the main course can range from something simple like *'Cheattie' Tarragon Chicken* to something more complex like *Roast Fillet of Beef with Shallots, Mushrooms and Red Wine Gravy*. In each case the basic rules stay the same. Firstly, go for the highest quality ingredients available to you before you plan your menu. If you have a first-class fishmonger buy fish, if you have a brilliant butcher buy meat, and remember that seasonal fruit and vegetables always offer better quality and value. Secondly, try to develop a good, basic cooking technique. Unfortunately, being a good cook doesn't come easily but practice makes perfect. So it's well worth rehearsing a dish before you serve it to your bank manager and his wife. And lastly, a carefully considered combination of ingredients makes all the differenece to the outcome of your main course, which is where this book might come in handy.

In order to achieve all of this the golden secret is planning! If the main course is to be part of a special meal plan it over a couple of days and make as much ahead as possible, for example all stocks and most sauces can be made ahead of time and frozen, and if you have a complex main make sure that your starters and desserts are nice and simple such as a soup and a dessert that will keep in the fridge. If your time is limited keeping a well-stocked store cupboard can make all the difference to the calibre of meals you produce.

Be adventurous: my recipes are simply guidelines, they're not set in stone. Don't be afraid to experiment and don't be afraid to cook something just because you've never done it before. You've got to start somewhere so, go on, get cooking!

Nick Nairn

# INGREDIENTS

### Celeriac
This large, knobbly swollen root has a pronounced nutty celery flavour and is available mainly in winter. Choose bulbs which are firm, heavy and without blemishes. Avoid buying very large bulbs, which can be tough and woody. Celeriac makes my favourite vegetable purée, and strangely, goes equally well with fish or game.

### Couscous
Couscous is semolina grains rolled, dampened and coated with fine wheat flour. A staple of North African cooking, it is a little bland on its own but a perfect vehicle for other flavours. As it is pre-cooked, it only needs to be moistened following the manufacturer's instructions. Once moistened, mix it with herbs, onions, chopped tomatoes or other ingredients and serve cold as a salad, although it is just as good hot.

### Grouse
The red or Scottish grouse, thought by many to be the finest of all game birds, is at its best from August to October. The shooting season, which starts on the Glorious Twelfth – 12 August – runs until 10 December. Young birds make the best eating and can be distinguished by soft downy breast feathers and pointed flight feathers at their wing tips. The spur at the back of the leg above the claws is also soft and rounded. Grouse are sold oven-ready (hung, plucked and drawn) in supermarkets. If you are lucky enough to have a butcher licensed to sell game nearby you can always have a go at preparing them yourself.

### Juniper berries
These small purply-black berries have an aromatic scent and a pine tang. They can be used fresh or dried – the dried berries have a stronger flavour than the fresh ones. The berries should be crushed with the back of a spoon, or with a pestle and mortar, to release maximum flavour. They have a particular affinity with game and are also used as a flavouring agent in gin.

### Maldon salt
This is a soft sea salt which can be crumbled between the fingers. It is not as coarse as normal sea salt and better by far than regular salt. (The men from Maldon haven't given me a bung for this, by the way, it has quite simply become an essential ingredient in my cooking.)

### Mallard (wild duck)
These are the largest – averaging about 1.1kg – most common wild ducks found for sale and are at their best in late autumn between October and December. Their flesh is lean and dark and inclined to be dry if not properly cooked, although there is a layer of fat under the skin.

### Pearl barley
One of the earliest cultivated cereals, barley is available in numerous forms. Pearl barley is a refined version of the grain. The husk is removed, then the barley is steamed, rounded and polished.

### Puy lentils
These lentils, from Puy in France, are tiny and grey-green and considered to be the most superior. They have a distinctive flavour, keep their shape and colour when cooked and make a delicious autumn or winter vegetable. They are delicious served with game stews.

### Savoy cabbage
These dark green, crinkly-leaved cabbages are normally available from November through to spring. Look for ones that are firm in the centre and feel heavy for their size.

### Sugar snap peas
These are a rounder and fuller shaped version of mangetout. They taste a little sweeter than mangetout and are cooked and eaten whole. Look for small, crisp bright specimens with fresh-looking stalks. Do not store for more than one to two days, well wrapped in polythene in the fridge.

### Sweet potatoes
These are not actually potatoes but tuber root vegetables. The skin can be pinkish or yellowish, while the flesh can range from mealy to moist and from white to orange in colour. Choose smooth, plump, small sweet potatoes with unwrinkled skins. Larger ones tend to be fibrous.

### White pepper
White pepper is made from fully ripened berries with their red skins and pulp removed. It is less hot and more aromatic than black pepper. I use white pepper with fish or white meat, black pepper with game or red meat.

# EQUIPMENT

### Cast-iron ribbed grill pan
This gives meat and vegetables a nice char-grilled flavour and the food looks good, too, especially if you turn it through a 90-degree angle after initial cooking to achieve an attractive crisscross pattern. There is no need to add oil to the pan, simply brush the food, if necessary, before cooking.

### Chinois sieve
A fine mesh, conical metal sieve which is very handy for straining stocks and sauces.

### Frying pans
The best are black iron. They are all-metal, which means they can be put straight into the oven. They need to be seasoned prior to use (not unlike a wok) and are superb for cooking with. They're also cheap and last for ever. However, if your budget will stretch to it, *good quality* stainless steel frying pans are fantastic.

### Hand-held blender
Also known as a 'stick liquidiser'. These small electric liquidisers have revolutionised sauce-making, allowing anyone to make light, frothy sauces and making 'split' sauces a thing of the past.

### Kilner jars
These swing-top jars with replaceable rubber seals are handy for storing Pesto, Tapenade, Home-dried Tomatoes and practically anything else you can cram into them. Give them a good old wash before use and ensure that anything kept in them is covered with olive oil.

### Knives
A large cook's knife (I use a 30cm/12in knife) and a flexible boning knife, combined with a good chopping board and a sharpening steel, will aid your cooking no end.

### Mandolin grater
Not essential, but very useful for larger quantities of slicing and grating and when very fine slices are required.

### Scone cutters
Buy the heaviest and strongest you can find. They are useful for cutting out Dauphinoise potatoes, shaping and many other things – including scones, I suppose.

1  Savoy cabbage
2  Celeriac
3  Fennel bulb
4  Sugar snap peas
5  Plum tomatoes
6  Red chillies
7  Rocket
8  Sweet potatoes
9  Chestnuts
10 Guinea fowl
11 Grouse
12 Duck breasts
13 Feta cheese
14 Goat's cheese
15 Scallops
16 Trout fillets
17 Couscous
18 Puy lentils
19 Pearl barley
20 Maldon salt
21 Juniper berries
22 White peppercorns
23 Chervil
24 Thyme
25 Tarragon

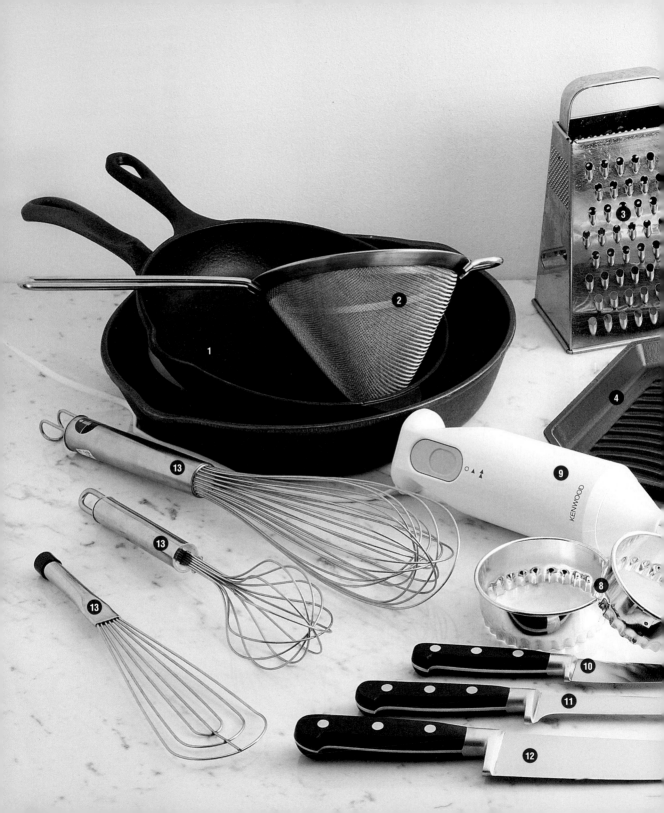

1. Black-iron frying pans
2. Chinois sieve
3. Box grater
4. Ribbed grill pan
5. Mandolin grater
6. Kilner jars
7. Slotted spoons
8. Scone cutters
9. Hand-held blender
10. Vegetable knife
11. Boning knife
12. Large cook's knife
13. Whisks

# Fish

## BAKED TROUT FILLETS WITH GLAZED LEEKS AND LEMON BUTTER SAUCE

This is delicious served with mashed potatoes. The leeks are cooked to the stage where they are almost falling in on themselves which intensifies and enriches their flavour. But they are not in any way heavy and work well with the delicate fish. The lemon butter sauce can also be served with many other fish dishes.

### Serves 4

70g/2½oz butter

350g/12oz large leeks, trimmed and cut into 2.5cm/1in pieces

juice and finely grated rind of 1 lemon

½ quantity Nage butter sauce (page 62)

4 skinless, boneless trout fillets each weighing about 140g/5oz (See Tip)

Maldon salt and freshly ground white pepper

1 Preheat the oven to 180C/350F/Gas 4. Place 40g/1½oz of butter in a small roasting tin, add the leeks and sprinkle with one teaspoon of lemon juice and plenty of seasoning. Cook in the oven for 45 minutes, turning a couple of times, then remove and keep warm. Increase the oven temperature to 230C/450F/Gas 8.

2 Add the lemon rind and one teaspoon of lemon juice to the Nage butter sauce, heat through, then keep warm.

3 Heavily grease a shallow ovenproof baking dish with some of the remaining butter. Season the trout and sprinkle with a little of the remaining lemon juice. Lay the trout fillets, skin-side down, on a work surface, then fold them in half across the middle so that they form a loop. Place in the baking dish and dot with the remaining butter. Add two tablespoons of water and bake the fillets for 6–7 minutes or until just cooked. (They should be firm, moist and rich and not overdone to a tasteless mush that refuses to stick to your fork.)

4 Divide the leeks between four warm plates and carefully place the trout fillets on top. Pour any juices from the trout baking dish into the butter sauce and give it a good whizz with a hand-held blender or a whisk, then pour it round the leeks.

**Nutrition notes per serving:** *492 calories, Protein 29g, Carbohydrate 3g, Fat 41g, Saturated fat 23g, Fibre 2g, Added sugar none, Salt 1.16g.*

### TIP

Trout is sadly an underused fish which has a terrific combination of great flavour and fine texture. Look for skinless, boneless Scottish trout fillets, preferably with the Scottish Quality Trout (SQT) symbol – not just because of the flavour but also because they come thoroughly boned.

# SHELLFISH RISOTTO WITH GINGER AND CORIANDER

This method removes the mystique from making risotto and allows you to finish it at the last moment. You can prepare the base up to a day in advance. Any shellfish combination will do. However, raw tiger prawns work well and are now found in many supermarkets. Do make sure these are fresh not frozen.

## Serves 4

1.8kg/4lb mussels, cleaned

200ml/7fl oz white wine

a little fish stock, if necessary

90ml/3fl oz olive oil, plus 1 tsp and extra, to serve

1 onion, finely chopped

2cm/¾in piece fresh root ginger, finely chopped

225g/8oz arborio rice

55g/2oz butter

50ml/2fl oz double cream, lightly whipped

25g/1oz Parmesan cheese, grated

meat of 3 scallops, sliced (optional)

115g/4oz cooked, peeled langoustine tails

2 tbsp Tomatoes concassé (See Tip)

1 tbsp roughly chopped fresh coriander, plus extra to serve

1 tsp fresh lemon juice

Maldon salt and freshly ground white pepper

Parmesan cheese shavings, to serve

1 Heat a large pan until very hot, then add the mussels and a quarter of the wine. Cover with a tight-fitting lid and cook for 3–4 minutes or until the mussels open. Remove the mussels from the pan using a slotted spoon. Discard any that do not open. Reserve the cooking liquid. Shell the mussels and chill. Strain the cooking liquid into a measuring jug and reserve. You will need 1 litre/1¾ pints so if it's a little short, make up the amount with fish stock.

2 Heat 90ml/3fl oz olive oil in a large frying pan, add the onion and ginger and sweat for 8 minutes or until soft. Add the rice and stir until it has absorbed the oil and become translucent. Stir in the remaining wine and six turns of the pepper mill. Stir for 4 minutes or until the wine has been absorbed.

3 Add 850ml/1½ pints of reserved mussel cooking liquid and bring to a simmer. Simmer for 10 minutes, stirring from time to time, then pour into a large sieve set over a bowl and reserve the liquid. Transfer the rice to a baking tray and rake flat. Leave to cool, then place in a plastic tub and chill.

4 To finish the risotto: place the rice, reserved rice-cooking liquid and the remaining mussel-cooking liquid in a pan. Bring slowly up to a simmer, stirring from time to time. As soon as the risotto starts to thicken (this takes about 4 minutes), add the butter and beat in well with a wooden spoon. Once it is fully incorporated, add the cream and grated Parmesan and keep beating.

5 Heat the teaspoon of olive oil and sear the scallops for 4–5 seconds on one side only. They should be slightly undercooked. Stir the scallops, langoustine tails, mussels, tomatoes, coriander and lemon juice into the risotto. Check seasoning and warm through for 2 minutes. It should be midway between soupy and stiff. If it is too thick, add a little more stock. Divide between warm bowls and sprinkle with Parmesan shavings, a little olive oil and coriander.

**Nutrition notes per serving:** *733 calories, Protein 28g, Carbohydrate 53g, Fat 43g, Saturated fat 16g, Fibre trace, Added sugar none, Salt 1.84g.*

## TIP

For the Tomatoes concassé: skin 2 ripe plum tomatoes. Slit a wee cross at the bottom of each tomato, pop into boiling water and leave for 30 seconds–1 minute depending on how ripe the tomatoes are. The skin should peel off easily. Cut into quarters, scoop out the seeds, then cut flesh into 5mm/¼in dice. These will keep up to 24 hours, but are best used immediately.

# BAKED FILLET OF HALIBUT WITH CABBAGE, SMOKED BACON AND A TARRAGON CREAM SAUCE

Halibut has sufficient flavour to partner the robust cabbage and bacon, which is all you really need for this dish. If you do want potatoes, however, I'd go for Rosti potatoes (page 59).

## Serves 4

1 small Savoy cabbage

1 tbsp olive oil

2 rashers smoked back bacon, cut into matchsticks

85g/3oz unsalted butter

4 x 140g/5oz skinless, boneless halibut fillets or steaks (See Tip)

2 tbsp dry white wine

Maldon salt and freshly ground white pepper

### FOR THE TARRAGON CREAM SAUCE

15g/½oz unsalted butter

2 shallots, sliced

4 button mushrooms, finely sliced

1 bay leaf

3 fresh tarragon sprigs, leaves stripped and chopped and stalks reserved

300ml/½ pint white wine

300ml/½ pint fish stock

300ml/½ pint double cream

fresh lemon juice, to taste

1 Make the sauce: melt the butter over a low to medium heat, then sweat the shallots and mushrooms until soft. Add the bay leaf and tarragon stalks, then increase the heat to high and add the wine. Reduce until it's nearly all gone.

2 Add the fish stock and reduce again until it's nearly all gone, then add the cream. Bring to the boil and strain through a fine sieve, forcing it through with the bottom of a ladle into a small clean pan. Season and add a few drops of lemon juice. Keep warm.

3 Preheat the oven to 230C/450F/Gas 8. Heat a medium pan until very hot. Peel off the coarse, outer leaves of the cabbage and discard. Give the centre a good wash, then cut it lengthways into quarters. Cut out the root part of each quarter, then finely shred the leaves with a sharp knife.

4 Pour the oil into the very hot pan and stir fry the bacon matchsticks until crispy. Add 25g/1oz butter, then the cabbage and stir fry for 5–6 minutes until tender. Season and keep warm.

5 Use 25g/1oz butter to grease the base of a roasting tin. Place the fillets or steaks in the tin, season with salt, pepper and lemon juice and dot the remaining butter over the fish, then pour over the wine.

6 Whack the tin into the oven and set the timer for 6 minutes. Place a good-sized pile of cabbage and bacon in the centre of each plate. Add the tarragon leaves to the sauce before pouring it round each pile of cabbage and bacon. If you are serving rosti, place one wedge on top of each pile, then top with a halibut fillet or steak. Spoon over any juices left in the roasting tin for extra flavour.

**Nutrition notes per serving:** *821 calories, Protein 31g, Carbohydrate 8g, Fat 69g, Saturated fat 38g, Fibre 4g, Added sugar trace, Salt 1.36g.*

### TIP

Halibut is an absolutely topping fish – it has a beautiful texture and flavour, it's easy to fillet and the bones make good stock. No scales to get everywhere either! Obviously designed by experts, this fish is readily available during the summer months – but you have to be careful not to overcook it, since it can become dried out very easily, due to its low fat content.

# SMOKED HADDOCK AND PUY LENTIL TART

### Serves 8

1 quantity Savoury flan pastry
(recipe below)

55g/2oz Puy lentils

300ml/½ pint double cream

675g/1½lb smoked haddock,
skin and bones removed
(finished weight 450g/1lb)

3 eggs, beaten

25g/1oz Parmesan cheese, grated

3 tbsp chopped fresh coriander

Maldon salt and freshly ground
white pepper

1  Preheat the oven to 200C/400F/Gas 6. Grease a metal 25cm/10in x 3cm/1¼in deep flan tin. Roll out the pastry to 3mm/⅛in thick and use to line the tin. Fill with greaseproof paper and baking beans and bake blind for 11 minutes. Remove the beans and paper and bake for 8–9 minutes until lightly golden. Remove from the oven and reduce the temperature to 190C/375F/Gas 5.

2  Meanwhile cook the lentils in slightly salted boiling water for 20–25 minutes until soft. Drain and leave to cool.

3  Bring the cream to the boil in a pan, then add the haddock. Cover and poach gently for 3 minutes, then remove from the heat and tip the contents into a large sieve set over a mixing bowl. Reserve the poaching liquid and break up the fish with a fork.

4  Leave the poaching liquid to cool, then mix in the eggs, lentils, Parmesan, coriander and flaked fish. At this stage, check and adjust the seasoning but do go easy on the salt.

5  Dump the whole lot into the pastry case and bake for 25 minutes, until just set. Cut into wedges and serve warm. It is nice served with a tomato salad.

**Nutrition notes per serving:** *555 calories, Protein 23g, Carbohydrate 26g, Fat 41g, Saturated fat 24g, Fibre 2g, Added sugar none, Salt 3.24g.*

### TIP

Always use good quality undyed smoked haddock (the flesh should be pale gold not red.) For an even richer, more luxurious tart you could substitute finely diced smoked salmon for the haddock. (Simply combine with the cream and remaining filling ingredients and cook the flan as above.)

# SAVOURY FLAN PASTRY

### Makes 1 x 25cm/10in flan

175g/6oz butter, diced

225g/8oz plain flour

1 tsp salt

1 egg, beaten

1  Rub the butter, flour and salt together in a bowl until the mixture has the consistency of fine breadcrumbs. Add the egg and bring it all together into a dough.

2  Knead the dough lightly five or six times with floured hands but stop if you feel it is becoming greasy, as this is the butter melting. Cover in plastic film and chill for 1 hour before use.

### TIP

In the summer months when the weather is hotter, reduce the amount of flour to 5oz and add 1 tablespoon of water to the butter and flour mixture when you add the egg.

# SEARED MACKEREL FILLETS WITH STIR-FRIED VEGETABLES AND A FROTHY BUTTER SAUCE

This is my favourite way to enjoy mackerel. One of my fondest memories of filming *Wild Harvest* on Skye is fishing for mackerel with Jerry Cox. Great shoals of mackerel filled the bay and we were able to walk out of Jerry's front door, straight on to his boat and catch our supper.

### Serves 4

55g/2oz fine green beans, halved

55g/2oz asparagus, cut into 5cm/2in lengths

4 spring onions, cut into 5cm/2in lengths

1 small courgette, cut into 5cm/2in batons

250g/9oz egg thread noodles

1–2 tbsp sunflower oil

4 mackerel fillets, each weighing 140g/5oz

juice of ½ lime

few drops Chilli oil (See Tip)

1 tsp Thai fish sauce (*nam pla*)

½ quantity Nage butter sauce (page 62)

15g/½oz finely chopped fresh coriander leaves

50ml/2fl oz double cream, lightly whipped

Maldon salt and freshly ground white pepper

1 Bring a pan of salted water to the boil. Add the green beans and bring back to the boil, then add the asparagus and bring back to the boil. Add the spring onions and courgette batons, bring back to the boil and drain immediately. Refresh under cold running water. Leave to drain on plenty of kitchen paper.

2 Bring a pan of salted water to the boil. Drop in the noodles, then remove the pan from the heat, cover and leave for 4 minutes. Drain and set aside. Add one teaspoon of sunflower oil so that the noodles do not stick together.

3 Heat a frying pan until it is really hot, add a splash of oil, then the mackerel fillets, skin-side down, and fry for 4 minutes. Turn over and fry for 2 minutes. Transfer to a plate, pour over half the lime juice, season and keep warm.

4 Heat a little oil in the pan, add the blanched vegetables and stir-fry for 1 minute, then add the Chilli oil, Thai fish sauce, remaining lime juice and seasoning.

5 Warm through the Nage butter sauce and whisk with a hand-held blender until light and frothy. Add the coriander and whisk, then whisk in the whipped cream.

6 Divide the noodles between four bowls, spoon on the vegetables, then top with the fish, skin-side up. Refroth the sauce, then spoon round the edge of the bowls.

*Nutrition notes per serving: 847 calories, Protein 36g, Carbohydrate 47g, Fat 58g, Saturated fat 23g, Fibre trace, Added sugar none, Salt 1.52g.*

### TIP

For the Chilli oil: slice 225g/8oz ripe red chillies in half lengthways and place in a large pan. Pour over 1 litre/1¾ pints sunflower oil and bring to the boil. Reduce heat and simmer for 5 minutes, remove from the heat and cool (this takes about 2 hours). Transfer the chillies and oil to a plastic tub with a lid and store in a cool place for 2–3 weeks. Pour the oil through a sieve to remove the chillies (or your oil will get too hot) and store in an old olive oil bottle. Remember to label it; a skull and crossbones will suffice.

**Warning! This stuff is mega, mega spicy and you'll have to take care not to get any in your eyes or other sensitive parts. Used sparingly, it imparts a wonderful glow to many dishes.**

# Poultry & Game

## 'CHEATTIE' TARRAGON CHICKEN

I adore chicken and tarragon. It's a marriage made in Scotland! But you could also try chervil, which has a milder flavour. In this recipe, I use chicken breasts (the 'Cheattie' part) which speeds up the cooking time to 20 minutes but you can make it in advance and reheat it (See Tip). Be careful not to overcook the chicken or it will dry out. Serve with new potatoes and a few lightly fried courgettes or other green vegetable.

### Serves 4

4 skinless chicken breast fillets

1 tbsp olive oil

55g/2oz unsalted butter

1 onion, diced

115g/4oz button mushrooms, halved

1 garlic clove, crushed

150ml/¼ pint white wine

300ml/½ pint chicken stock or a chicken stock cube

150ml/¼ pint double cream

15g/½oz fresh tarragon leaves

Maldon salt and freshly ground white pepper

few drops fresh lemon juice, to serve

1 Season the chicken breasts. Heat a large frying pan until it is hot, then add the olive oil and butter and whack in the chicken. Cook for 2–3 minutes on each side until nicely browned.

2 Add the onion, mushrooms and garlic and stir well, chasing them around the pan to absorb the juices and prevent them from burning. Once the onion has started to soften, add the wine, which should boil off fairly quickly, then add the stock and reduce over a high heat. Turn the chicken breasts a couple of times to ensure they cook evenly.

3 When the stock has become very thick, add the cream and tarragon and boil again. Check the seasoning and add a few drops of lemon juice before serving on a bed of green beans.

**Nutrition notes per serving:** *484 calories, Protein 28g, Carbohydrate 4g, Fat 36g, Saturated fat 20g, Fibre trace, Added sugar none, Salt 0.77g.*

### TIP

If you are keeping the dish for any length of time don't add the tarragon. Remove the chicken from the heat, cover it with a butter wrapper to prevent a skin from forming and leave to cool. Add two tablespoons of water and the tarragon before reheating thoroughly.

# ROAST BREAST OF GUINEA FOWL WITH SEARED VEGETABLES AND A TAPENADE SAUCE

I would go for mashed potatoes, Dauphinoise (page 56) or sautéed new potatoes with this dish.

## Serves 4

1–2 tsp salt

1 small aubergine, cut into 8 slices

4 guinea fowl breasts, skin on
(See Tip)

olive oil, for frying

50g/2oz butter

fresh lemon juice

2 medium courgettes, each cut into
4 x 45 degree angled slices

1 Roasted red pepper, quartered
(page 56)

Maldon salt and freshly ground
white pepper

FOR THE SAUCE

55g/2oz unsalted butter

2 shallots, thinly sliced

4 button mushrooms

1 bay leaf

1 fresh thyme sprig

300ml/½ pint red wine

300ml/½ pint chicken stock

200ml/7fl oz double cream

1–2 tbsp Tapenade (page 60)

1 Preheat the oven to 230C/450F/Gas 8. Lightly salt the aubergine slices and leave to drain for 15 minutes, then wash and drain in a sieve.

2 Make the sauce: heat a medium pan, add 25g/1oz butter and when it sizzles, add the shallots, mushrooms, bay leaf and thyme and fry until golden. Add the wine and reduce until nearly dry, then add the stock and reduce by two-thirds. Stir in the cream and Tapenade. Bring to the boil, sieve into a pan; keep warm.

3 Heat a large ovenproof frying pan until hot and season the guinea fowl breasts. Add one tablespoon of olive oil to the hot pan, with the remaining butter. When the butter starts to brown, add the guinea fowl breasts, skin-side up, and cook for 2 minutes. Turn over and cook for 3–4 minutes until the skin is dark brown.

4 Add one teaspoon of lemon juice and place the pan in the oven for 2 minutes. Remove and turn the guinea fowl to skin-side up and rest in a warm place.

5 Heat a frying pan until hot and pat the aubergine slices dry. Pour a 3mm/⅛in depth of olive oil into the pan and add the aubergine slices. Fry until nearly black, turn over and fry other sides. Place on a warm metal tray and keep warm.

6 Tip the oil out of the pan, discard, then replace with two tablespoons of fresh oil. Add the courgette slices, cut faces down, and cook for 2–3 minutes until browned. Season with Maldon salt, four turns of pepper and one teaspoon of lemon juice and stir until well coated. Transfer to the tray with the aubergines. Stir fry the pepper quarters in the pan, then season with salt, pepper and lemon juice. Cook for 1 minute, add to the vegetable tray and keep warm.

7 Pop the pan with the guinea fowl back into the oven for 90 seconds to reheat, then cut each breast into three slices. Check sauce for seasoning. Divide the vegetables between plates and spoon round the sauce. Arrange the guinea fowl, skin-side up. Skim fat from pan juices and drizzle juices over each breast.

**Nutrition notes per serving:** *816 calories, Protein 22g, Carbohydrate 7g, Fat 72g, Saturated fat 32g, Fibre 3g, Added sugar none, Salt 1.61g.*

## TIP

A lot of people are suspicious of guinea fowl because it's unfamiliar. They needn't be – it's similar to chicken, only tastier, with a faint, gamey tang and real flavour. If you get a chance to get some, go for it.

# TRADITIONAL ROAST GROUSE

The best way to appreciate the unique flavour of grouse is to serve it simply without fancy sauces and garnishes – a perfectly cooked bird accompanied by bread sauce and game gravy is all that is required. Serve with a bowl of rowan jelly and plain boiled potatoes.

## Serves 4

½ onion, studded with 3 cloves

5 bay leaves

5 fresh thyme sprigs

1 garlic clove, crushed

100g/3½oz unsalted butter

300ml/½ pint milk

12 juniper berries

4 young oven-ready grouse

4 slices bread

90ml/3fl oz clarified butter (See Tip)

300ml/½ pint red wine

1 tbsp cassis

600ml/1 pint game stock

2 tbsp sunflower oil

175g/6oz fresh breadcrumbs

Maldon salt and freshly ground white pepper

fresh watercress, to serve

1  Start the bread sauce: place the onion, one bay leaf, a thyme sprig, the garlic, 55g/2oz of unsalted butter and milk in pan and bring to the boil. Simmer for 5 minutes, remove from the heat and leave to infuse.

2  Place three juniper berries, one thyme sprig and one bay leaf into the cavity of each bird, then smear the outside of each bird with 25g/1oz unsalted butter and keep them in the fridge until you are ready to cook them.

3  Make the *croûtons*: using a scone cutter stamp out 4 x 6cm/2½in discs of bread. Heat the clarified butter and gently shallow fry the discs until golden. Drain on kitchen paper and reserve.

4  Make the gravy: combine the red wine, cassis and stock in a pan and reduce until it starts to thicken. Whisk in 15g/½oz of butter, season and keep warm.

5  Preheat the oven to 230C/450F/Gas 8. Heat a 30cm/12in black-iron frying pan until it is very hot. Add the sunflower oil and place the birds, breast-side down, in the pan and cook for 2 minutes. Turn them on to their other breasts and cook for 2 minutes – their breasts should now be nicely browned.

6  Turn the birds on to their undersides and place the pan in the oven and cook for 8 minutes. Remove pan and stand in a warm place for at least 10 minutes.

7  Finish the bread sauce: strain the milk into a clean pan, add the breadcrumbs and whisk over a medium heat for 2–3 minutes until thickened. Season well.

8  Warm the *croûtons* and gravy in the oven and check the seasoning. Place a *croûton* on a warmed plate, sit a grouse on top and fill its cavity with watercress. Dollop some bread sauce beside the bird and pour over some gravy.

**Nutrition notes per serving:** *1013 calories, Protein 60g, Carbohydrate 54g, Fat 57g, Saturated fat 29g, Fibre 2g, Added sugar none, Salt 2.48g.*

## TIP

For clarified butter: melt 250g/9oz unsalted butter in a small pan over a low heat. Allow to stand for a few minutes until all the oil rises to the top, then skim off the oil into a sealable plastic container. Discard the watery buttermilk. This makes about 200ml/7fl oz and will keep for 2 months. You can buy it ready prepared in Indian delicatessens (where it is called ghee).

# PAN-FRIED PHEASANT BREAST WITH CARAMELISED APPLES, CHESTNUTS AND A CIDER AND CHERVIL SAUCE

The main problem with cooking pheasant is that (like pigeon) it has a very low fat content and is prone to becoming dry, especially if overcooked. This dish has a nice creamy sauce which moistens it. I use vacuum-packed chestnuts – not quite as good as the real thing, but a hell of a lot easier. I like to eat this with roast potatoes.

### Serves 4

4 skinless pheasant breasts

55g/2oz unsalted butter

1 tsp icing sugar

2 Granny Smith apples, peeled, cored and quartered

16 small button mushrooms

300ml/½ pint dry cider

300ml/½ pint chicken stock

300ml/½ pint double cream

16 vacuum-packed chestnuts

2 tbsp roughly chopped fresh chervil

Maldon salt and freshly ground white pepper

1 Season the pheasant breasts. Heat a large frying pan until it is hot, then add half the butter. When it's foaming, add the pheasant breasts and cook for 3 minutes on each side until lightly coloured. Remove from the heat and keep warm.

2 Add the remaining butter and the icing sugar to the pan, then add the apples and gently fry for 3–4 minutes. Remove the apples and keep warm.

3 Add the mushrooms to the pan, increase the heat to high and stir until they absorb the butter. Add the cider and reduce until it is all gone. Add the stock and reduce by four-fifths. Stir in the cream and bring back to the boil.

4 Return the pheasant breasts and apples and any juices to the pan. Add the chestnuts and warm everything through for 3 minutes. Add half the chervil and season the sauce. Place the pheasant breasts on warmed plates, spoon the chestnuts, apples, mushrooms and the sauce over them, then sprinkle with the remaining chervil.

**Nutrition notes per serving:** *774 calories, Protein 36g, Carbohydrate 24g, Fat 58g, Saturated fat 30g, Fibre 2g, Added sugar 1g, Salt 0.86g.*

### TIP

Pheasant comes into season in October, but it's best to wait until December, since the price falls dramatically (and the birds are nice and plump!).

# COLD ROAST CHICKEN WITH FETA CHEESE, ROSEMARY, LEMON AND OLIVE OIL

Perfect for a picnic or an al fresco summer lunch, or as a winter starter to remind you of summer. This relies on good ingredients to make a simple dish great. Try to get a good free-range chicken to roast and buy the best feta you can find. This is definitely an excuse to use your top-of-the-range olive oil. You can even make this dish up a day in advance as the flavours improve over time. Serve with a few dressed salad leaves and a drizzle of olive oil.

### Serves 3–4

1.5kg free-range chicken

55g/2oz butter

175g/6oz feta cheese, crumbled into small pieces (See Tip)

leaves from 1 fresh rosemary sprig, finely chopped

50ml/2fl oz olive oil

finely grated rind of I lemon

3 tbsp fresh lemon juice

Maldon salt and freshly ground white pepper

1   Try to roast the chicken a day ahead. Preheat the oven to 200C/400F/Gas 6. Push your fingers between the chicken breast and the skin to make two pockets. Stuff 15g/½oz butter into each one and rub the remaining butter all over the outside of the skin.

2   Season well and place the bird on a wire rack over a roasting tin. Bang it into the oven and roast, basting from time to time, for about 1 hour or until well browned. Depending on your oven, you might need to cover the chicken loosely with a sheet of foil after 40 minutes to stop it from over-browning before it is cooked through.

3   To test that the chicken is cooked, insert a skewer in the thickest part of the thigh: the juices should run clear. Leave until cold, then pull off the legs and use a knife to cut off the breasts. Ferret out the two oysters from the underside (these are little secret crackers of flesh). Using your fingers, flake the flesh from the breasts, thighs, drumsticks and oysters. Try to get nice long strands and don't forget the skin.

4   Pile all the flaked chicken into a large bowl and add the feta. Whisk together the rosemary leaves, olive oil, lemon rind and juice and some seasoning and add to the bowl. Toss well, check the seasoning and keep cold until needed.

**Nutrition notes per serving for three:** *1110 calories, Protein 82g, Carbohydrate 1g, Fat 87g, Saturated fat 34g, Fibre none, Added sugar none, Salt 3.4g.*

### TIP

Feta cheese is a traditional ewe's milk cheese, originally from Greece, which is now more commonly made from cow's milk. It is preserved in brine which may account for its salty flavour which tends to increase with age. It is brilliant white with a firm, crumbly texture and is normally sold in vacuum packs.

# PAN-FRIED DUCK WITH STIR-FRIED GREENS AND A WHISKY, SOY, HONEY AND LEMON SAUCE

The secret of success here is to get the sweet and sour balance in the sauce just right. If you can get hold of them, you could use mallard breasts instead of duck (See Tip).

4 small boneless duck breasts

sunflower oil, for frying

6 spring onions, cut into strips

85g/3oz fine green beans, halved and blanched

85g/3oz asparagus, blanched

85g/3oz sugar snap peas, blanched

Maldon salt and freshly ground white pepper

**FOR THE WHISKY, SOY, HONEY AND LEMON SAUCE**

600ml/1 pint chicken stock

2 tbsp whisky

1 tbsp good heather honey

1 tbsp light soy sauce

1 tbsp fresh lemon juice

25g/1oz butter, diced

1   Make the sauce: boil the stock vigorously until reduced to 125ml/4fl oz. Add the whisky, honey, soy sauce, lemon juice and seasoning and set aside.

2   Season the duck breasts well. Heat a large frying pan until very hot, add a good splash of sunflower oil, then the breasts, skin-side down. Cook for 4–5 minutes until crisp and brown. Cook the other sides for 2 minutes, leaving the centres pink. Remove and leave in a warm place for 10 minutes.

3   Add a little extra oil to the pan, if necessary, then add the spring onions, beans, asparagus and peas and stir-fry over a high heat for 1–2 minutes. Season well.

4   Bring the sauce back to the boil, lower the heat and whisk in the butter a little at a time. Check the seasoning. Carve each breast diagonally into slices. Place the vegetables on four warm serving plates, arrange the duck on top, then pour over the sauce.

**Nutrition notes per serving:** *777 calories, Protein 20g, Carbohydrate 8g, Fat 72g, Saturated fat 21g, Fibre 1g, Added sugar 4g, Salt 1.16g.*

Mallard are the largest of the wild ducks, and have a really special flavour. It's really important to rest them after they have been cooked – this is the stage that ensures that the breasts become really tender, it also allows the colour inside the meat to even out.

# POT-ROAST CHICKEN PAPRIKA ❄

This is one of the first things I ever cooked in my basement flat in Byres Road, Glasgow. Apart from spaghetti bolognese and chilli con carne, it was the first dish I had made with any degree of success. Nostalgia aside, it's a very tasty staple that freezes very well. The better the paprika the better the dish, so either go to a reputable wholefood store or make friends with a Hungarian. You can buy boneless chicken thighs if you prefer. This is fine served on its own but is also very good with pasta or new potatoes.

### Serves 4

8 chicken thighs

2 tbsp sunflower oil

25g/1oz butter

1 onion, sliced

1 garlic clove, crushed

1 large red pepper, seeded
and cut into 5mm/¼in dice

1 tsp paprika

1 tsp redcurrant jelly

200g can chopped tomatoes

1 tsp tomato purée

½ tsp chopped fresh thyme leaves

600ml/1 pint chicken stock

350g/12oz potatoes, cut into
1cm/½in dice

2 tbsp Shallot and tarragon butter
(See Tip)

Maldon salt and freshly ground
white pepper

4 tbsp crème fraîche and 2 tbsp
snipped fresh chives, to garnish

1  Preheat the oven to 180C/350F/Gas 4. Bone the chicken thighs: run a sharp knife down the thigh bone, cutting into the meat to allow it to come away. Do this several times on each side until the bone comes free. Cut each thigh into four even-sized pieces.

2  Heat a large frying pan until very hot. Add the oil and enough pieces of chicken to just cover the base of the pan – don't crowd it or the temperature will drop and the chicken will end up stewing. Fry over a high heat, turning now and then, until golden. Season well and spoon into a casserole dish. Fry any remaining chicken the same way.

3  Add the butter to the frying pan, together with the onion, garlic, red pepper and paprika, and fry for 5 minutes. Add the redcurrant jelly, chopped tomatoes and tomato purée and cook for 2 minutes. Stir in the thyme and stock. Season well and simmer for 5 minutes. Pour over the chicken pieces and stir in the potatoes. Cover with a tight-fitting lid and bake for 35 minutes, until the chicken and potatoes are tender.

4  Stir in the Shallot and tarragon butter until melted, then serve in warmed bowls garnished with the crème fraîche and chives.

**Nutrition notes per serving:** *600 calories, Protein 31g, Carbohydrate 25g, Fat 43g, Saturated fat 15g, Fibre 3g, Added sugar 2g, Salt 1.32g*

❄ *This can be frozen for up to 1 month. Defrost thoroughly then reheat until piping hot.*

### TIP

For the Shallot and tarragon butter: melt 25g/1oz butter in a pan, add 115g/4oz chopped shallots and cook over a gentle heat for 5–6 minutes or until the shallots are very soft but not coloured. Leave to cool, then beat into 200g/7oz softened butter, together with 25g/1oz finely chopped fresh tarragon and fresh lemon juice and seasoning to taste. Spoon the mixture on to a sheet of plastic film and shape into a 2.5cm/1in thick roll. Wrap well in plastic film and chill in the fridge for a week or freeze for up to 2 months. Always make this well in advance so that it has enough time to harden.

# ROAST CHICKEN LIVERS AND BACON WITH PARMESAN AND CHIVE MASH AND GRAVY

This is liver, bacon and onions with knobs on. Each ingredient has been given a little extra to make this an addictively tasty dish that also makes a good starter. Chicken livers are one of the last remaining cheap luxury items, and I can't seem to get enough of them. The mash, too, is rich and creamy and marries well with the sweet, textured gravy.

## Serves 4

2 tbsp olive oil

4 rindless streaky bacon rashers, halved

350g/12oz chicken livers, thawed if frozen and trimmed

Maldon salt and freshly ground white pepper

**FOR THE GRAVY**

4 tsp red wine vinegar

1 tbsp redcurrant jelly

400ml/14fl oz chicken stock

2 tbsp Red onion marmalade (page 62)

**FOR THE MASH**

450g/1lb potatoes, cut into chunks (See Tip)

40g/1½oz butter

25g/1oz Parmesan cheese, finely grated

1 tbsp snipped fresh chives, plus long cut chives, to garnish

1  Make the gravy: place the vinegar and redcurrant jelly in a small pan and leave over a gentle heat until the jelly has melted. Increase the heat and boil until thick. Add the chicken stock and boil until reduced by half. Stir in the Red onion marmalade and boil until it has reduced to 150ml/¼ pint and thickened. Season well, set aside and keep warm.

2  Make the mash: cook the potatoes in boiling salted water until tender. Drain well. Return to the pan and mash with the butter until smooth. Stir in the Parmesan, snipped chives and seasoning, then set aside and keep warm. It will keep for up to 1 hour.

3  Heat a large frying pan until very hot, then add the olive oil and bacon rashers and fry for 1–2 minutes on each side, until the rashers are crisp and golden. Set aside and keep warm.

4  Season the chicken livers well, add to the pan (don't crowd the pan, cook in batches if necessary) and cook for just 1 minute on each side. You want the outsides to become lightly browned but the insides to remain pink and juicy.

5  Pile the mash into the centres of four warmed plates, spoon over the chicken livers, then top with two pieces of crisp bacon. Spoon the gravy around the outside and garnish with the chives.

**Nutrition notes per serving:** *466 calories, Protein 25g, Carbohydrate 26g, Fat 30g, Saturated fat 12g, Fibre 2g, Added sugar 5g, Salt 1.92g.*

### TIP

Mashed potatoes are a great comfort food. The secret of success lies in the quality and type of potatoes used (preferably Maris Piper, Pentland Squire or King Edward). Older spuds work better than new – and make sure they are thoroughly cooked, but not soggy!

# *Meat*

## ROAST LEG OF LAMB WITH GARLIC AND ROSEMARY BAKED IN FOIL

During the filming of the *Wild Harvest* television series, top gamekeeper Ronnie Rose showed me how he cooked a leg of roe deer wrapped in foil – and it was absolutely delicious. It was cooked for 2 hours and so was well done – not normally how I like my roast meat, but on this occasion I was converted. Here I have used a leg of lamb and added a few more flavours – but the idea belongs to Ronnie. Serve with Dauphinoise potatoes (page 56).

### Serves 8

3kg leg of lamb, trimmed (See Tip)

115g/4oz unsalted butter

12 garlic cloves

3 fresh rosemary sprigs

2 onions, quartered

300ml/½ pint red wine

25g/1oz Maldon salt, crushed

12 turns freshly ground white pepper

1 Preheat the oven to 190C/375F/Gas 5. Line a roasting tin with enough foil to fold over and cover the lamb, then place the lamb on the foil in the tin. Melt the butter in a small pan, then bring it to the boil.

2 Scatter the garlic and rosemary over the lamb and place the onion quarters around it. Pour the wine over the lamb and sprinkle with the salt and pepper. Pour the boiling butter over the lamb, seal everything inside the foil and bang the tray into the oven for 3 hours.

3 Remove the lamb from the oven and leave to relax for 30 minutes in a warm place. Open up the foil and lift out the lamb. Divide the onion quarters and garlic bits (which will be dark and squidgy) between eight plates, then strain off the juices into a pan, reheat, and check the seasoning. Carve the lamb.

**Nutrition notes per serving:** *733 calories, Protein 57g, Carbohydrate 4g, Fat 52g, Saturated fat 27g, Fibre trace, Added sugar none, Salt 3.61g.*

### TIP

Scottish lamb is wonderful. Try to get the native blackface or Shetland breeds. It's at its best from spring to summer – from about the end of May until mid-September – after which it develops a more mutton-like flavour.

# PEPPERED FILLET OF BEEF WITH STRAW SWEET POTATOES AND A SALAD OF HERBS

This is a simple dish but a real masterpiece. The pale pinky-orange sweet potatoes give it a welcome twist. The steak is fried, then coated in buttery, meaty juices. Just that. Heaven.

## Serves 4

3 tbsp black peppercorns

4 x 175g/6oz fillet steaks

4 tsp Dijon mustard

675g/1½lb pink sweet potatoes

sunflower oil, for deep frying

25g/1oz clarified butter (See Tip, page 27)

55g/2oz unsalted butter

50ml/2fl oz Armagnac or Cognac

4 tbsp beef stock

3 tbsp double cream

Maldon salt and freshly ground white pepper

Salad of herbs, to serve (See Tip)

1 tbsp olive oil

1 tsp lemon juice

1 Crush the peppercorns coarsely in a coffee grinder. Tip the pepper into a fine sieve and shake out all the powder, which would make the steaks far too spicy. Spread the peppercorns over a small plate. Smear both sides of the steaks with the mustard and coat in the peppercorns. Season with salt (salting first would prevent the pepper sticking to the meat) and set aside.

2 Cook the straw sweet potatoes: use a mandolin to cut the potatoes into narrow strips about 3mm/⅛in thick. Wash in cold water, then place in a clean tea towel and wring out as much moisture as you can. Pour 2.5cm/1in of sunflower oil into a large deep pan or wok and heat to 180C/350F or use a deep-fat fryer. Drop the potatoes into the hot oil, a few at a time. (Don't throw them in all at once or the oil will boil over.) Fry for 5–6 minutes, stirring from time to time, until pale golden. Drain on kitchen paper and season. The pototoes can be kept warm in a low oven for 30 minutes.

3 Heat a large frying pan until hot. Add the clarified butter, then the steaks and give them a couple of minutes on each side (a bit longer if you don't like your meat rare). Do not move them around in the pan or the peppercorn crust will fall off. Add the unsalted butter and allow it to colour to nut brown, basting the steaks as you go. Transfer the steaks to a baking tray. Leave in a warm place.

4 Add the Armagnac or Cognac to the pan and boil over a high heat for 1 minute – the alcohol must be boiled off. Add the stock, bring the mixture back to the boil and pour in the cream. Scrape and stir together any gooey bits from the bottom of the pan. When the sauce boils, it is ready. Pour any steak juices into the sauce, place a steak on each plate, then spoon over the sauce. Serve with a pile of salad and the straw potatoes.

**Nutrition notes per serving:** *772 calories, Protein 39g, Carbohydrate 42g, Fat 48g, Saturated fat 20g, Fibre 4g, Added sugar none, Salt 0.99g.*

### TIP

For the Salad of herbs: season 25g/1oz mixed fresh herbs with a pinch of salt and four turns of the white-pepper mill. You can vary the herbs but I always return to the following combinations: basil, flatleaf parsley and rocket; chervil, tarragon and fennel; and chives, dill and chervil. Divide into nice sprigs and keep in a bowl covered with plastic film in the fridge. Drizzle over one tablespoon of olive oil and one teaspoon fresh lemon juice and toss to coat. Serve immediately.

# SPICED PORK FILLET WITH APPLES, RAISINS AND CALVADOS

Pork fillet is lean and good value but just a little bland. I've tried to perk it up here, in what is quite a substantial and spicy dish. You can save time by using ready-ground spices (but See Tip). Serve with boiled new potatoes and green vegetables.

## Serves 4

450g pork fillet, trimmed and cut across into 2.5cm/1in wide pieces

3 tbsp sunflower oil

25g/1oz butter

1 small onion, finely chopped

1 tsp ground cinnamon

½ tsp ground allspice

½ tsp ground ginger

1 tbsp light muscovado sugar

50ml/2fl oz Calvados

55g/2oz raisins

2 Granny Smith apples, peeled, cored and cut into 1cm/½in dice

150ml/¼ pint chicken stock

150ml/¼ pint double cream

Maldon salt and freshly ground white pepper

### FOR THE SPICE COATING

2 tbsp plain flour

1 tbsp light muscovado sugar

2 tsp salt

2 tsp ground cinnamon

1 tsp English mustard powder

1 tsp each of ground cumin, ground coriander, crushed black peppercorns, ground allspice and freshly grated nutmeg

1 Lay a few pieces of pork fillet at a time between two sheets of plastic film or dampened greaseproof paper. Using a rolling pin, carefully beat them out until they are about 5mm/¼in thick. Don't be too vigorous or your slices of pork will begin to fall apart.

2 Mix together all the ingredients for the spice coating and spread out on a large plate. You will have more than you need but it will keep in a sealed plastic bag until the next time you want to use it.

3 Heat a large frying pan until hot, then add the oil. Coat a few slices of the pork in the spice mixture and fry for 2 minutes on each side or until cooked through and lightly golden. Lift out on to a plate and keep warm while you cook the remaining pork.

4 Lower the heat under the frying pan and add the butter. When it has melted, add the onion, cinnamon, allspice, ginger and sugar and fry for 5 minutes or until the onion has softened. Stir in the Calvados, raise the heat and bring to the boil, scraping up any bits that have stuck to the bottom of the pan.

5 Add the raisins and apples and cook for 2–3 minutes, then add the stock and boil until reduced by half. Add the cream, bring to the boil and cook for 1–2 minutes until the sauce has thickened. Check the seasoning. Return the pork and any juices to the pan and simmer until the pork has heated through.

**Nutrition notes per serving:** *648 calories, Protein 27g, Carbohydrate 38g, Fat 41g, Saturated fat 19g, Fibre 2g, Added sugar 8g, Salt 3.25g.*

## TIP

Beware of using ready-ground spices. They don't last as long as many of us think. The golden rule is to buy little and often, and store them in an air- and light-tight container. We grind all our spices to order at the restaurant, using a coffee grinder. It's well worth the effort.

# ROAST FILLET OF BEEF WITH SHALLOTS, MUSHROOMS AND RED WINE GRAVY

Do make the effort to get Aberdeen Angus! Ask your butcher to cut the fillets from the centre of the fillet and get him to trim off the gristle and 'chain' and give you the meaty trimmings.

### Serves 4

1 tbsp sunflower oil, for frying

4 x 140g/5oz slices beef fillet
(See Tip), reserve trimmings

20 whole peeled shallots,
reserve trimmings

1 fresh thyme sprig

1 bay leaf

5 black peppercorns, bruised

300ml/½ pint red wine

200ml/7fl oz chicken stock

200ml/7fl oz beef stock

85g/3oz cold unsalted butter,
plus extra for frying

1 tbsp icing sugar

fresh lemon juice

20 nice pieces mushroom
(chanterelle or morel, but whole
brown button will do)

2 tbsp beef fat

Maldon salt and freshly ground
black pepper

**1** Make the gravy: heat a large frying pan, add the sunflower oil and fry the beef trimmings until browned. Add the shallot trimmings, thyme, bay leaf and crushed peppercorns and cook over a medium heat until nicely coloured. Pour in the wine and slosh it around before reducing it until all the liquid has gone.

**2** Add both the stocks and gently simmer for 30 minutes or until thickened. Pass the gravy through a fine sieve and leave to stand. Skim the fat off the top.

**3** Poach the shallots in boiling salted water for 10 minutes or until tender, then drain. Fry in 25g/1oz of butter with the odd dusting of icing sugar and continue cooking over a low to medium heat until the shallots are a good golden brown. Keep warm or reheat in the oven. Season and add lemon juice before serving.

**4** Heat a large frying pan until hot and add 25g/1oz of butter. Fry the mushrooms for 4–5 minutes until browned. Season with salt, pepper and lemon juice. The mushrooms can be cooled and reheated.

**5** For four steaks you will need two pans. Season the steaks well. Heat the pans until very hot and add one tablespoon of beef fat or of a sunflower and butter combination to each. The fat or oil should smoke. Quickly add the steaks and get some colour on them – 2 minutes on each side if you want them good and rare. For medium or more well-done steaks, place them in a hot oven after sealing and cook until done to your liking. Allow the steaks to relax in a warm place for a minimum of 10 minutes or a maximum of 30 minutes (when they will need 90 seconds or more in a hot oven to reheat).

**6** Place each steak on a bed of spinach. Arrange the shallots and mushrooms around them. Add the remaining butter to the gravy and reheat. Season the gravy, then pour it over and around the meat and the shallots and mushrooms.

**Nutrition notes per serving:** *504 calories, Protein 32g, Carbohydrate 10g, Fat 32g, Saturated fat 16g, Fibre 1g, Added sugar 5g, Salt 0.95g.*

### TIP

Without doubt, pure-bred Aberdeen Angus beef, properly treated and hung for at least 21 days, is the best beef you can buy. Running a close second are Galloway, Shorthorn and Highland cows. However, even the meat from a continental cross animal, when properly hung, will be fine for this dish.

# Vegetarian Dishes

## LASAGNE OF ROASTED RED PEPPERS, HOME-DRIED TOMATOES, OLIVES, CAPERS AND A BASIL BUTTER SAUCE ⓥ

*One of my repertoire of vegetarian main courses. As usual, fresh pasta is better than dried. When you serve it to your guests, listen out for murmurs of the '...who needs meat?' variety.*

### Serves 4

**3 large Roasted red peppers, diced into 5mm/¼in squares (page 56)**

**8 pieces Home-dried tomatoes (page 60)**

**16 black olives, stoned and halved**

**20 salted capers, rinsed and drained**

**25ml/1fl oz olive oil**

**1 tsp Chilli oil (See Tip, page 20)**

**fresh lemon juice**

**175ml/6fl oz Nage butter sauce (page 63)**

**25g/1oz fresh basil leaves, roughly torn**

**Eight 10x10cm/4x4in lasagne sheets, cooked**

**25g/1oz Parmesan cheese shavings**

**Maldon salt and freshly ground white pepper**

1  Preheat the oven to 110C/225F/Gas ¼. Place the peppers, tomato pieces, olives, capers, olive oil and Chilli oil in an ovenproof pan, then season with salt, pepper and lemon juice. Gently warm through over a medium-low heat for 10 minutes. Cover and keep warm (for up to 1 hour) in the oven.

2  Bring a pan of salted water up to a simmer, and in a separate pan warm through the Nage butter sauce. Add two-thirds of the basil to the sauce, which miraculously now becomes basil butter sauce. Check the seasoning.

3  Drop the lasagne sheets into the simmering water and heat through for 60 seconds. Remove using a slotted spoon and leave to drain on a clean tea towel.

4  Lay out four warm shallow serving bowls. Place one sheet of lasagne flat on the bottom of each, and wrinkle by pushing the opposite ends together. Top with an eighth of the pepper mixture. Cover with another lasagne sheet and divide out the remaining pepper mixture. Spoon over the basil butter sauce, then scatter over the Parmesan shavings and remaining basil.

**Nutrition notes per serving:** *379 calories, Protein 8g, Carbohydrate 32g, Fat 25g, Saturated fat 9g, Fibre 4g, Added sugar none, Salt 1.59g.*

### TIP

You could vary the ingredients, substituting roast courgettes or aubergine for the peppers. Or try rocket, flatleaf parsley or chives in the sauce.

# NORTH AFRICAN COUSCOUS WITH ROAST VEGETABLES Ⓥ

Just a handful of spices combine with a basic range of fresh ingredients to produce this kaleidoscopic and many-layered dish. Preserved lemons can be found in many delicatessens.

## Serves 4

1 large aubergine, cut lengthways into 1cm/½in thick slices

1 tsp each of ground cumin, ground cinnamon, ground coriander, ground allspice

25g/1oz butter

1½ tsp light muscovado sugar

40g/1½oz pine nuts, toasted

85g/3oz raisins

425ml/¾ pint Nage (page 62) or water

2 tbsp chopped fresh coriander

250g/9oz couscous

few slices of preserved lemon, finely chopped (optional)

1 red onion, thickly sliced

1 red and 1 yellow pepper, seeded and quartered

1 large courgette, sliced lengthways

125ml/4fl oz olive oil, plus extra for grilling

2 shallots, finely diced

2 plum tomatoes, chopped

1 tbsp fresh lemon juice

Maldon salt and freshly ground white pepper

1 Place the aubergine slices in a colander, salt well and leave for 30 minutes. Rinse well then pat dry.

2 Mix together all the ground spices. Melt the butter in a large pan that has a tight-fitting lid, add three teaspoons of the spices and the sugar and fry over a low heat for 1–2 minutes. Add the pine nuts, raisins, Nage or water and half the coriander and bring to the boil. Add the couscous, stir, then cover and remove from the heat. Leave for 5 minutes, stirring half-way through, until the couscous is light and crumbly. Season and add the preserved lemon, if using. Keep warm.

3 Heat a ribbed grill pan until very hot. Use cocktail sticks to hold the layers of onion slices together, if necessary. Grill the onion, peppers, courgette and aubergine slices a few at a time with plenty of olive oil and seasoning on both sides until well coloured and tender.

4 Meanwhile, make the sauce: heat the remaining spices in a small pan, then add 125ml/4fl oz of olive oil and the shallots and cook over a low heat for 5 minutes until the shallots are soft. Add the chopped tomatoes, the remaining coriander and the lemon juice and season well.

5 Pile the couscous on to warm plates with a tower of roast vegetables on top. Reheat the sauce, if necessary, and spoon it round the couscous.

**Nutrition notes per serving:** *723 calories, Protein 9g, Carbohydrate 61g, Fat 51g, Saturated fat 9g, Fibre 6g, Added sugar 2g, Salt 0.78g.*

## TIP

To simplify the dish, you can omit the sauce and serve the couscous and vegetables with just olive oil drizzled around them.

# CELERY AND PARMESAN TART Ⓥ

### Serves 8

1 quantity of Savoury flan pastry
(See Tip, page 19)

350g/12oz celery, finely diced
(See Tip)

300ml/½ pint double cream

3 eggs, beaten

85g/3oz Parmesan cheese, grated

2 tbsp finely snipped fresh chives

Maldon salt and freshly ground
white pepper

1  Preheat the oven to 200C/400F/Gas 6. Roll out the pastry and use it to line a 25cm/10in greased flan tin and bake blind as on page 19. Remove from the oven and reduce the temperature to 190C/375F/Gas 5.

2  Mix together all the remaining ingredients in a bowl and season well. Pour into the pastry case and bake for 30 minutes or until just set. Don't overcook the filling, it should still be slightly wobbly in the centre. Cut into wedges and serve warm with a tomato and herb salad.

**Nutrition notes per serving:** *514 calories, Protein 11g, Carbohydrate 23g, Fat 43g, Saturated fat 26g, Fibre 1g, Added sugar none, Salt 1.64g.*

### TIP

The secret of this tart is to cut the celery very, very finely, as it isn't precooked. It should still have a crunch to it and the filling should be soft and cheesy. The celery could be chopped in a food processor, but for best results do it by hand. Peel it first to get rid of any tough fibres.

# BRAISED ROOT VEGETABLES WITH PEARL BARLEY AND TARRAGON Ⓥ

### Serves 4

25g/1oz butter

3 tbsp olive oil

1 onion, cut into large chunks

2 each of carrots, celery sticks, leeks, large potatoes and parsnips, cut into large chunks

¼ swede, cut into large chunks

40g/1½oz pearl barley

2 tsp tomato purée

1 tbsp plain flour

600ml/1 pint Nage (page 62)

2 tbsp chopped fresh tarragon

Maldon salt and freshly ground
white pepper

1  Heat the butter and olive oil in a large pan. When the butter is foaming, add the vegetables and stir fry over a high heat until well browned. Add the pearl barley and tomato purée and cook for 2–3 minutes.

2  Stir in the flour and seasoning, then gradually stir in the stock. Cover and simmer for 25 minutes. Check that all the vegetables are tender, then add the tarragon and simmer for 1 minute. Check the seasoning before serving

**Nutrition notes per serving:** *325 calories, Protein 6g, Carbohydrate 44g, Fat 15g, Saturated fat 4g, Fibre 6g, Added sugar none, Salt 1g.*

# GOAT'S CHEESE SOUFFLÉ Ⓥ

Good goat's cheese from forward-thinking independent cheesemakers is becoming more accessible through specialist shops, delicatessens and supermarkets. Its fine, deep flavour and interesting texture sets it apart from its factory-produced counterparts. You need a ripe cheese for this.

## Serves 4–6

**40g/1½oz butter**

**2 tbsp fresh white breadcrumbs**

**2 tbsp finely grated Parmesan cheese**

**25g/1oz plain flour**

**300ml/½ pint milk**

**leaves from 2 small fresh thyme sprigs, finely chopped**

**4 eggs, separated**

**225g/8oz ripe goat's cheese, such as Saint Maure, crumbled**

**Maldon salt and freshly ground white pepper**

1 Heavily grease an 18cm/7in soufflé dish with 15g/½oz of butter. Mix the breadcrumbs with the Parmesan and use it to coat the inside of the dish – the butter will help the soufflé to rise and the breadcrumbs and Parmesan form a nice crust. Chill.

2 Preheat the oven to 180C/350F/Gas 4. Melt the remaining butter in a pan, add the flour and cook gently for 1 minute to form a roux. Meanwhile, warm the milk in another pan, then gradually whisk into the roux, season and add the thyme. Bring the mixture to the boil, stirring, then lower the heat and simmer very gently for 15 minutes – the surface should be barely moving.

3 Transfer the sauce into a large bowl, cool for 10 minutes, then beat in the egg yolks and goat's cheese. This is the soufflé base. If you are not baking it immediately, dot the top with butter to prevent a skin forming.

4 Whisk the egg whites in a large, clean bowl until they form soft peaks. The tips of the peaks should flip over slightly, not stand upright.

5 Spoon a quarter of the egg whites into the soufflé base and stir them in to loosen the mixture, then, using a large metal spoon, gently fold in the remaining egg whites. It doesn't matter if there are a few lumps of white in the mixture.

6 Spoon the mixture into the soufflé dish, then tap the base gently on a hard surface to level the top. Bake for 28–30 minutes until well risen and golden. You can check near the end of cooking but, whatever you do, don't open the oven door in the first few minutes. Serve the soufflé straight from the oven. It may crack slightly on top, but don't worry, this is all part of its charm.

**Nutrition notes per serving for six:** *256 calories, Protein 13g, Carbohydrate 11g, Fat 18g, Saturated fat 6g, Fibre trace, Added sugar none, Salt 1.13g.*

### TIP

If you can't find, or don't like, goat's cheese, this soufflé is excellent made with Gruyère, Parmesan or a good sharp Cheddar.

# GATEAU OF ROAST VEGETABLES WITH SAUCE VIERGE, PESTO AND TOMATO VINAIGRETTE Ⓥ

This looks spectacular with its two sauces and the vegetables can always be roasted in advance.

### Serves 4

1 large aubergine, cut into 8 rounds

100ml/3½fl oz olive oil

1 medium fennel bulb

fresh lemon juice

4 medium courgettes,
cut lengthways into 4 strips

2 Roasted red peppers, quartered
(page 56)

2 ripe plum tomatoes, quartered

125ml/4fl oz Mediterranean sauce
vierge (See Tip)

25g/1oz rocket leaves

2 tbsp Pesto (page 60)

Maldon salt and freshly ground
white pepper

1 Preheat the oven to 200C/400F/Gas 6. Lightly salt the aubergine rounds and drain in a colander for 15 minutes. Rinse well, drain for at least 45 minutes, then pat dry. Fry the aubergine slices in olive oil until golden brown. Trim and quarter the fennel.

2 Heat a black-iron frying pan until it is hot, add two tablespoons of olive oil, then the fennel. Lightly fry until browned. Season with salt, pepper and lemon juice, then pour in 600ml/1 pint water. Bring to the boil and reduce by three-quarters. Place in the oven for 10 minutes. The fennel should be tender and most of the water absorbed. Reduce the temperature to 160C/325F/Gas 3.

3 Meanwhile, in another pan heat two tablespoons of olive oil. Add the courgette slices and cook for 2–3 minutes until browned. Season with salt, four turns of pepper and one teaspoon of lemon juice and stir until coated. Stir fry pepper quarters in the pan, then season with salt, pepper and lemon juice and cook for 1 minute. Cool all the vegetables in the fridge if not using immediately. Liquidise the tomatoes with 30ml/1fl oz olive oil. Sieve into a bowl and season.

4 Assemble each gateau: place two courgette strips on a baking sheet, then place two aubergine rounds on top, then two pepper quarters. Add two more strips of courgette and top with a fennel quarter. Warm in the oven – about 20 minutes if the vegetables have been chilled. In two small pans warm through the sauce vierge (See Tip) and the vinaigrette, but don't let either boil.

5 Place the rocket leaves in a bowl, drizzle with lemon juice and remaining olive oil, season and toss. Place a gateau on each plate, and pour a couple of spoonfuls of tomato vinaigrette round it. Add the pesto to the sauce vierge and spoon this round the plates. Top the gateaux with the rocket leaves.

Nutrition notes per serving: *629 calories, Protein 5g, Carbohydrate 12g, Fat 63g, Saturated fat 9g, Fibre 6g, Added sugar none, Salt 1.42g.*

### TIP

For 175ml/6fl oz Mediterranean sauce vierge: place 200ml/7fl oz extra virgin olive oil, 115g/4oz finely chopped shallots, one lightly crushed (but still whole) garlic clove, one fresh thyme sprig, one bay leaf, one teaspoon crushed Maldon salt and 12 turns of white pepper in a small pan. Warm through gently for 20 minutes until the sauce is hot but not boiling. Remove from the heat, add 25ml/1fl oz sherry vinegar and cool. Remove the bay leaf, thyme and garlic.

# *Vegetables*

## ROASTED RED PEPPERS Ⓥ

### Serves 4

6 red peppers

olive oil, for preserving

1 garlic clove

1 thyme sprig

1 bay leaf

1 The secret is to get the pepper skin blackened without burning the flesh underneath. This can be done in three ways. Grilling: turn the grill to high, drizzle a little olive oil over the peppers and place under the grill, turning as the skin blackens. Baking: preheat the oven to 240C/475F/Gas 9. Place the peppers in a shallow roasting tin at the top of the oven and turn as they blacken. Skewered over a gas burner – my favoured method: prong the peppers on a skewer and place directly over a burner on a gas cooker, turning as they blacken. I use a blowtorch to finish off any stubborn patches.

2 Once the skins are totally blackened, wrap in plastic film and cool. Unwrap and wash off the skins with water. Slice into quarters and remove and discard the pith and seeds.

3 Use immediately or store in a Kilner jar, pouring in enough olive oil to cover. Add the garlic, thyme and bay leaf for flavour. The peppers will keep for up to two weeks in the fridge.

**Nutrition notes per drained pepper :** *125 calories, Protein 2g, Carbohydrate 10g, Fat 9g, Saturated fat 1g, Fibre 3g, Added sugar none, Salt 0.02g.*

## DAUPHINOISE POTATOES Ⓥ

### Serves 8

1 garlic clove crushed with ½ tsp Maldon salt

300ml/½ pint full cream milk

300ml/½ pint double cream

8 turns freshly ground white pepper

½ heaped tsp Maldon salt

1.25kg/2¾lb potatoes, preferably Maris Piper

25g/1oz Parmesan cheese, grated

1 Preheat the oven to 150C/300F/Gas 2. Place the garlic and salt in a large pan with the milk, cream and pepper. Bring to the boil. Thinly slice the potatoes on a mandolin (or in a food processor). Place them in the pan and stir to coat in the cream and milk mixture.

2 Bring to the boil and simmer, stirring gently once or twice, for about 15 minutes until the potatoes are tender, and the mixture has thickened. Turn into a buttered ovenproof dish, leaving any burnt slices on the bottom of the pan.

3 Sprinkle with the Parmesan and bake for 1 hour or until nicely browned on top. Serve immediately or cool overnight.

**Nutrition notes per serving:** *325 calories, Protein 6g, Carbohydrate 30g, Fat 21g, Saturated fat 13g, Fibre 2g, Added sugar none, Salt 1g.*

### TIP

To reheat, cut the potatoes into squares or use a 6cm/2½in scone cutter to make rounds. Lift the rounds out of the cutter, place on a baking tray and pop them into an oven preheated to 140C/275F/Gas 1 oven for 45 minutes.

# CELERIAC VEGETABLE PURÉE Ⓥ

**Serves 8**

**450g/1lb celeriac**

**850ml/1½ pints milk**

**55g/2oz butter**

**Maldon salt and freshly ground white pepper**

1 Cut off the top and bottom of the celeriac and cut the bulb into quarters. Peel the quarters (take off slices about 5mm/¼in thick) and cut each one into eight pieces. Place in a pan, just cover with milk and season. Bring to the boil, then simmer for 15–20 minutes or until tender.

2 Strain though a sieve set over a mixing bowl. Reserve the milk. Place the celeriac in a food processor with the butter and about four tablespoons of reserved milk and purée for 3–4 minutes until very smooth. Check the seasoning.

**Nutrition notes per serving:** *131 calories, Protein 4g, Carbohydrate 6g, Fat 10g, Saturated fat 6g, Fibre 2g, Added sugar none, Salt 0.66g.*

### VARIATIONS

For carrot purée: use water instead of milk. Cook 450g/1lb carrots for 20–30 minutes or until very tender and add a tablespoon of fresh lemon juice to the cooking water. Continue as above.

For beetroot purée: wear rubber gloves to peel 450g/1lb beetroot, then cook them in water instead of milk for 45 minutes–1 hour. Continue as above.

# ROSTI POTATOES Ⓥ

**Serves 4**

**450g/1lb potatoes**

**90ml/3fl oz clarified butter (See Tip, page 27)**

**½ tsp Maldon salt**

**6 turns freshly ground white pepper**

1 Grate the potatoes, using a box grater, on to a clean tea towel, then wring out any excess moisture by twisting the towel into a tight ball shape. Place the potatoes in a bowl, add 25ml/1fl oz of clarified butter and season.

2 Heat the remaining butter in a 20cm/8in frying pan, and add the potatoes, pushing them down with a spatula to evenly cover the pan. Cook over a medium heat for 8–10 minutes until you see traces of colour at the edges, then turn the potatoes over and cook for 3–4 minutes until they are golden on both sides. Drain on a wire rack, cool and cut into quarters.

**Nutrition notes per serving:** *251 calories, Protein 3g, Carbohydrate 19g, Fat 19g, Saturated fat 12g, Fibre 2g, Added sugar none, Salt 0.64g.*

### TIP

The rosti can be made up to 6 hours in advance and left at room temperature until ready to use. Reheat in an oven preheated to 180C/350F/Gas 4 for 5 minutes.

# Basic Recipes

## PESTO ✳

The traditional version of this sauce uses only basil leaves. I like to vary it by using a combination of flatleaf parsley, rocket and basil.

| Makes about 425ml/ ¾ pint |
|---|

**85g/3oz mixed fresh basil, flatleaf parsley and rocket leaves**

**55g/2oz Parmesan cheese, grated**

**55g/2oz pine nuts**

**2 garlic cloves, roughly chopped**

**1 tsp Maldon salt**

**12 turns freshly ground white pepper**

**200ml/7fl oz virgin olive oil**

1 Place all the ingredients in a food processor and whizz for 30 seconds. Scrape around the inside with a plastic spatula and whizz again for 30 seconds. That's it.

2 Scoop into a Kilner or screwtop jar and store in the fridge for up to two weeks. Each time you use some pesto, flatten down the surface with a broad spoon and splash on some more olive oil. This helps to keep it sealed and stops it darkening and losing its flavour.

✳ *Freeze the pesto in ice-cube trays and either keep covered with plastic film or transfer the cubes to a sealed tub once frozen. It should keep for up to 3 months.*

## HOME-DRIED TOMATOES

These are a sweet and plump version of what usually come in jars labelled 'sun-dried tomatoes'. It is important to use really good ripe plum tomatoes. Around 12 hours of oven time is involved in making these, so it's a good idea to do them overnight. It's worth it – they are a taste sensation.

| Makes 24 halves |
|---|

**12 large ripe plum tomatoes**

**Maldon salt, crushed**

**12 turns freshly ground white pepper**

**50ml/2fl oz olive oil, plus extra for preserving**

**1 fresh basil or thyme sprig**

**1 garlic clove, crushed**

1 Preheat the oven to 110C/225F/ Gas ¼. Slice each tomato in half, through the growing eye at the top, then remove the green eye. Lay the tomatoes on a baking sheet, cut-sides up and sprinkle lightly with salt and pepper. Drizzle with the olive oil.

2 Place in the oven and leave for 8 hours. The tomatoes should be reduced to half their original size but not browned. Turn over and cook for 4 hours until firm. Remove from the oven and cool.

3 Place in a Kilner jar and add a basil or thyme sprig and the garlic and cover with olive oil. The tomatoes can be stored in the fridge for up to three weeks.

## TAPENADE

This is a classic Provençal olive, caper and anchovy sauce – great on toast, pizzas, roast courgettes, aubergines and fennel. The tuna helps to make it milder and I love it dolloped on to fresh tomato soup.

| Makes about 425ml/¾ pint |
|---|

**55g/2oz can anchovy fillets, drained**

**2 garlic cloves**

**175g/6oz pitted olives**

**55g/2oz can tuna in oil, drained**

**55g/2oz capers (dried and salted rather than in brine, washed)**

**juice of ½ lemon**

**leaves from 1 fresh thyme sprig**

**1 bay leaf**

**125ml/4fl oz olive oil**

**1 tbsp brandy**

1 Place all the ingredients in a food processor and whizz for about 2 minutes. Scrape into a Kilner jar or sealable, air-tight tub. This will keep for four weeks in the fridge.

## NAGE (MARINATED VEGETABLE STOCK) ✿

This stock is essential when making Nage butter sauce, so make big batches when you can.

**Makes 1.2 litres/2 pints**

**1 large onion and 1 leek, chopped into 1cm/½in dice**

**2 celery sticks, chopped into 1cm/½in dice**

**1 fennel bulb, chopped into 1cm/½in dice**

**4 large carrots, chopped into 1cm/½in dice**

**1 head garlic, sliced in half across its equator**

**8 white peppercorns, crushed**

**1 tsp each of pink peppercorns and coriander seeds**

**1 star anise**

**1 bay leaf**

**40g/1½oz mixed fresh herbs**

**300ml/½ pint white wine**

1  Place all the vegetables in a large pan and cover with water. Add the garlic, peppercorns, coriander seeds, star anise and bay leaf, bring to the boil and simmer for 8 minutes. Add the fresh herbs and simmer for 3 minutes.
2  Add the wine and remove from the heat. Cover and marinate for 48 hours in a cool place. Strain through a fine sieve and use the stock immediately or freeze.

✿ *This stock freezes well. Freeze in 600ml/1 pint tubs and defrost when needed. It can be frozen for up to six weeks.*

## NAGE BUTTER SAUCE

This sauce is my own favourite and the one I use most in my cooking. A hand-held blender is essential when making it – without one, it is difficult to obtain the light, smooth quality which makes it so versatile.

**Makes about 300ml/½ pint**

**600ml/1 pint Nage**

**200g/7oz unsalted cold butter, diced**

**1 tsp fresh lemon juice**

**pinch of salt**

**4 turns freshly ground white pepper**

1  Pour the Nage into a straight-sided pan, filling slightly more than half the pan. Place over a high heat and bring to the boil, then reduce to roughly one-fifth of its original volume. (It turns dark and looks thick and sticky.)
2  Turn the heat to low and add all the butter. Using the hand-held blender whisk until all the butter has melted and the texture is light and frothy. Add the lemon juice, salt and pepper and keep warm (don't let it boil) until it's needed.
3  If you let the sauce go cold and it solidifies, you can melt it but the butter will float to the top. Boil 90ml/3fl oz double cream and whisk with the blender. While whisking the cream, pour in the hot 'split' sauce in a steady stream. And, hey presto, lovely light sauce.

## RED ONION MARMALADE

The natural sweetness of red onions gives this a mellower flavour than ordinary onions would. The marmalade is great with cold meats, game, chicken livers and bacon. Or add a tablespoon to gravy to make a rich onion gravy.

**Makes 500g/1lb 2oz**

**90ml/3fl oz olive oil**

**1.3kg/3lb red onions, finely sliced**

**125ml/4fl oz best quality sherry vinegar or, even better, cabernet sauvignon vinegar**

**2 tbsp crème de cassis**

**Maldon salt and freshly ground white pepper**

1  Heat the oil in a large pan over a medium heat. Add the onions and stir to coat, then season. Cook the onions slowly, uncovered, stirring from time to time, until they are very soft and the sugary juices have caramelised. This should take about 1–1½ hours and the onions should look thick, dark and sticky.
2  Add the vinegar and cassis and cook for 10 minutes or until all the harsh vinegar has been boiled off and the marmalade has a glossy texture. Cool, then store in a jar in the fridge. If you pour in a tablespoon of olive oil to seal the top it should keep for six to eight weeks.

**Other Titles in the *TV Cooks* Series include:**

Michael Barry Cooks Crafty Classics
Mary Berry Cooks Cakes
Mary Berry Cooks Puddings & Desserts
Keith Floyd Cooks Barbecues
Sophie Grigson Cooks Vegetables
Valentina Harris Cooks Italian
Ken Hom Cooks Chinese
Madhur Jaffrey Cooks Curries
Rick Stein Cooks Fish

**The following videos in the *TV Cooks* Series are available:**

Michael Barry Cooks Crafty Classics
Mary Berry Cooks Cakes
Mary Berry Cooks Puddings & Desserts
Sophie Grigson Cooks Vegetables
Valentina Harris Cooks Italian
Ken Hom Cooks Chinese
Nick Nairn Cooks the Main Course
Rick Stein Cooks Fish

# INDEX